CARPOOLING WITH GOD

By
Loren T. Taylor

Carpooling with God
by Loren T. Taylor

Printed in the United States of America

ISBN 978-1-60477-877-9

Unless otherwise indicated, Bible quotations are taken from The New International Version. Copyright © 1973, 1978, 1984 by Zondervan Publishing House.

www.xulonpress.com

.

This book is dedicated to the memory of my father,

William Henry Taylor

who taught me that being sensitive,
feeling and caring
is what makes a man truly strong!

TABLE OF CONTENTS

INTRODUCTION

"You can accomplish more in one hour with God than one lifetime without him." - God's Little Instruction Book

In my office I have a rolltop desk that I like to tape little scraps of paper to with phone numbers, clippings, and little notes to myself. One clipping that has been there now for a number of years that is anonymous, and is entitled,

"So Far Lord." It reads:
"Dear Lord, so far today I've done all right. I haven't gossiped, haven't lost my temper, haven't been greedy, grumpy, nasty, selfish, or over-indulgent.

I'm very thankful for that. But in a few minutes, Lord, I'm going to get out of bed.

And from then on, I'm probably going to need a lot more help!"

I have kept this little piece of paper in front of me on my desk as a reminder. To me, one of the biggest challenges that I face each day is how I remain true to myself, and more importantly to God, each week as I go out to do battle in the business world.

For me, being true to my religious and moral beliefs in the workplace has always been my biggest test. How do I continue to be true to my personal beliefs when I find myself confronted by a situation where I am faced with behavior that, in my opinion, is ethically and sometimes morally corrupt? When you are raised as a Christian, to be truthful and ethical and above moral corruption, the challenge can be great. How do you respond to situations where people around you are being rewarded for behavior that you cannot possibly condone? When people are doing anything possible to get ahead no matter whom it hurts or what rules have to be broken? In my career I have found myself so repulsed by the behavior of management in a company that I quickly found a new job and left.

After leaving this one job in particular, I watched for years as one of the most morally and ethically corrupt people that I have ever met rose to stardom with the company, and even graced the cover of magazines like Fortune and Business Week. This person basked in the limelight for many years and then finally made a big mistake and had his star fall quickly. As a Christian, I felt sorry for this individual, but inside I also felt this sense of relief that there is justice in this good world of ours. I have always felt that being able to look at one's self in the mirror each morning and see an honest face is the most important thing.

There are many, many pressures on everyone in the workforce. Money can make people do certain things that they wouldn't ordinarily do. There are things that I have done in my career that I now look back on and am less than proud of. The desire to get that promotion or raise, or to close that deal can push anyone to cut a few ethical corners. The simple truth is that you cannot hide from the fact that you are responsible for your actions no matter who you are. You are not your job; you are a person with beliefs and principles. As Bill O'Reilly wrote: "Right is right and wrong is wrong. You can look it up in the Bible or the Koran."

What I have resolved for myself is that each and every day I shall try to be the best person I can be, and lead by example. I can't change other people or live their lives for them. What I can do is to live my own life and try to be a positive influence on others. I try to hold myself up to very close scrutiny. To never lie and to do things that I know are right no matter what the consequences. I am not perfect and like everyone I make mistakes and fall backwards at times, but to know that God is there to pick me up when I need the help is a very powerful feeling. I believe that each person can make a big difference in the world each day by trying hard to only do the right things and to let people know that God is guiding them.

Changes don't just miraculously happen. Suddenly a switch does not turn on that makes everything better. It is a long and tedious task and it is won, one battle at a time. It has become so much simpler since I started to *carpool with God*. You can too. God is everywhere! Just open your heart and He will be there for you. All you need to do is *ask* God to ride with you to work each morning and be with you throughout the day and He will. God is interested in each and every one of us and wants us all to succeed.

A recent report by the Conference Board showed that only 45% of Americans are satisfied with their jobs. In a *Business Week Online* article, a poll was quoted that found that American managers want a deeper sense of meaning and fulfillment on the job even more than they want more money and time off. This is a very significant finding as *Business Week* also reported that people are working the equivalent of over a month more each year than they did a decade ago.

A recent study by the Gallup Organization said that three in four Americans would like to see religious beliefs play a bigger role in people's lives. Eight in ten said they wished that their faith were stronger. To be fulfilled, we have to be true to ourselves. As Robert Schuller wrote, "Our work consumes at least half of our waking life. How can we exclude God from half of our life and be personally and professionally successful? We can't check God at the door when we go to work." In other words, we must utilize our spiritual beliefs to guide our business decisions.

I've struggled with this battle for many years and during some periods was more successful with it than during others. Years ago, I wrote a prayer entitled "Carpooling With God" that I keep on a folded up piece of paper in my wallet. I wrote it to help guide me through my daily struggles in the working world. I've tried to read it each day as I was commuting to work or during challenging times, whether in my office, on a train, a bus, or in a hotel room. It is the basis of this book. I will share it with you at the end.

Carpooling With God is a simple story written about a character named Jim Fletcher who inadvertently invites God to come to work with him each day. Its message is simple and clear. If you use your "inner spiritual voice" to guide you each day, you will find fulfillment and harmony that you never knew existed. Jim faces many unique challenges in his life. However, through God's guidance the necessary actions he needs to take become very clear.

People are sometimes too quick to predict their long-term happiness strictly based on a short-term end result. You cannot truly measure yourself only by what you have achieved. More important is what you as a person have become in the process. As is written in *God's Little Instruction Book*, "A person's true character is revealed by what he does when no one is watching." Have you been true to your spiritual self? If you listen to God's *advice* and utilize it to enhance your many talents you will be more successful than you ever imagined.

The pressure on the average worker grows with each year. With record layoffs happening in corporations all across America, the burden on the remaining workers continues to build. One's job has taken on an even bigger role, with most of us spending more time working than time with our families. Therefore, the quality of the time at work has become even more critical. Recent corporate ethics scandals have shaken the very core of American business. People are not sure where to turn. The best response is to not turn at all and simply *invite* God along to be by your side. He will gladly share your burden. God will never desert you. He will always light the way for you if you let Him. Would the crisis at Enron have occurred if all of the top executives had been carpooling with God? I believe not!

I would like to suggest that you start each morning thinking that this and every day is a gift from God that you have been blessed with. Feel empowered, for you now have God as your personal partner. *Listen* to His *advice* and *guidance* and use it wisely. Be a complete person at your job. For me, as a Christian, the definition of God is self-evident. To you, God may mean Allah, Khuda, Brahman, Atman, Great Spirit, the "higher being" or simply "spirituality." You can personalize the Message or the Messenger to suit your own beliefs.

Carpool with God each and every day and there is nothing that can stop you. There are no lane restrictions when you *Carpool With God*. Several years ago, the U.S. Department of Transportation Federal Transit Administration reported that Americans lose more than 1.6 million hours a day stuck in traffic. That was over a decade ago—imagine what the figure must be today. So, use your time wisely and cherish every minute to prepare for your day and share this precious time with God. Start out with God each morning and *ask* Him to stay with you all day long.

"with God all things are possible."
Matthew 19:26

Chapter One - FINDING YOUR PURPOSE

*"There is a place that you are to fill and no one else
can fill, something that you are to do,
which no one else can do."* - Plato

*"It's never too late to become what you might have
been."* - George Eliot

It was a Friday morning that seemed like any other. Jim Fletcher got dressed, came downstairs to fill up his travel coffee mug, pick up his briefcase and he was off. He yelled goodbye to his wife and kids and went to the garage to get in his car and drive the 30 minutes (traffic cooperating) to work.

Recently, Jim had become a bit ambivalent about work. An empty feeling had come over him. For most of his career as an executive with the Foremost Real Estate Company he had always been excited about going to work. He had been the ultimate company man, pushing to make the next quarter's numbers, leaving no stone unturned. Turn up the heat, damn the torpedoes. Whatever the company needed him to do he would do. The company came first and would always take care of him. Now he found himself coming up with excuses to continually postpone certain job responsibilities that he found to be less than stimulating. Or he'd delegate them to others, knowing they wouldn't do as good of a job as he would.

On Sunday, after his usual morning trip to church, Jim spent the rest of the day with his wife of ten years, Emily, and their two sons Mark and Eric, going out for a family picnic at a local park. It had been a very nice weekend. On Sunday night, Jim sat alone in his den in his favorite chair just thinking. Something was missing that he couldn't explain. He was 37 years old and happily married with a nice home and a job that paid very well. They weren't exceptionally rich, but lived a comfortable upper-middle class life. However, something was just not right. He felt empty and didn't know why, so he did something he hadn't done in a long time. He got down on his knees to pray. He asked for guidance and direction to help give his life meaning, and to make things at work fulfilling again, and to settle some issues that had become bothersome to him. He then got up and went to bed.

Monday morning brought the same old routine. Jim popped his trunk with his remote, plopped his briefcase inside, then closed it and opened the front door and got in. He put his travel mug in its holder, buckled up, put the car in reverse and backed out of the garage. He got out of the driveway and onto the street, put his car in Drive, and started his trip to work.

"Good morning Jim," a soft, soothing Voice next to him said.

Utterly startled, Jim momentarily lost control of his car, swerving left then right before getting it back under control. In the front passenger seat, a diaphanous form faded in and out of view. At first it was a voice only, but Jim quickly began to feel an energy presence that for a second would take on a human shape, then disappear—sort of like when you are trying to tune in an out-of-range radio station. Soon, there was no mistaking that a front seat passenger had miraculously materialized. It was an elderly, wizened man wearing what appeared to be all-white loose-fitting clothes. His radiant face was like none other that Jim had ever encountered in the chaotic world of business. This man's countenance asserted that He was completely and absolutely at peace with Himself, like the classic pictures of Jesus.

Jim could feel the hairs on both arms sticking straight up. He shook his head violently, and slapped his face with his hand, hoping that would rid him of his eerie passenger. But the apparition remained, staring straight ahead, once again softly speaking.

"You're going to run a stop sign if you're not careful, Jim."

Jim whipped his head to front, simultaneously stamping on the brakes and bringing the car to rest just inches short of a crosswalk. A plump and feisty School Crossing Guard was thrusting a hand-held stop sign in Jim's direction. She shot him a stern look that demanded, 'pay attention!' Satisfied that the driver got the message, she waved to her charges to begin their crossing. As twelve third graders made their way across the street, each one in turn paused to stare at the careless driver. Not a one of them gave even the briefest glance at his conspicuous Passenger.

When Jim turned to his right he understood why. His Passenger had somewhat "dematerialized." There was still a faint outline of Him, but in effect, He had become as clear as glass. To Jim, He appeared to be sort of a shimmering liquid glass. Clearly, He was indistinguishable to everyone else. But one thing was unmistakably clear and resonant: The Voice.

"Don't you just love children?"

"Who are you and what are you doing here?" Jim cautiously asked.

"I think that you know who I am, Jim." This was not just any voice. Soft but profound, it seemed to be coming from no particular direction—or all directions at once. It had a miraculous soothing quality, but nonetheless caused Jim's skin to prickle each time He spoke. "You prayed for My guidance last night, remember?"

"You've gotta be kidding!" Jim's heart was pounding like a hammer. "Who put you up to this?" Occasionally a practical joker himself, Jim looked into his backseat, half expecting to see one of his coworkers hunkered down and smirking with delight.

"Jim, you asked for My help and here I am," the Voice assured him. "You are important to Me, Jim. I care about you and am here to assist you. Whenever someone asks Me for help, I am always there."

The angry honking of a horn startled Jim almost as much as the Voice had. A glance at his rearview mirror revealed a perturbed driver. The children were well out of the cross-walk so Jim took his foot off the brake and eased on down the street. Feeling befuddled, Jim shrugged his shoulders. "But I've prayed for guidance before and You never showed up."

"Yes I did," the Voice corrected him kindly. "You just didn't recognize Me. Certainly you must know that I can assume any form I choose, or communicate any way that I wish. Sometimes, My answer to your prayer will be in a song lyric on the radio. Perhaps it is one word on a bill-board you are passing by. I might speak to you through a friend of yours. I communicate with you all the time, but you seldom listen — seldom pick up on the cue, so to speak. I may attempt to communicate to you through a stranger on the street—whom you choose to ignore. I am always communicating with all of you, but many of you are too caught up in your hectic lives to notice. In fact, I'm *always* speaking to you, but you, and most other people for that matter, simply do not pay attention. And now, for reasons of My own, I've decided to communicate with you directly—one-on-one to use a sports term you are familiar with.

Jim momentarily wondered how the Voice knew about his frequent use of the phrase, but quickly figured it out. "But... but why me of all people? Why here and now? And why are you being so... so *obvious* this time?"

"Because you asked, is all I will say for now," the Voice allowed. "But don't worry, Jim, everything will become clear to you in time."

Jim maneuvered into the lane that would become his freeway on-ramp, ascended the short incline, and merged into traffic.

"Well," Jim said nervously, "what do we do now?"

"Let's just talk," the Voice said. "It'll take you twenty minutes to get to work, so we have some time for you to tell Me about what is troubling you."

Jim was overwhelmed by this proposal. His mouth was open, but no words came forth. Finally, he gained his composure and decided what he wanted to say. "Well, I am just not happy these days and by most people's standards I should be." He scratched his head, merging into the "fast" lane.

Typical for a Monday, traffic was crawling at 20 – 30 m.p.h. "I have everything that just about anyone would want in life, but I still feel empty. I don't even enjoy my job the way I used to. I just don't feel good about it now. I don't know what is going on and I don't know what to do about it."

"Jim, may I ask you something?"

"Of course," Jim answered, surprised his permission was being solicited with such loving earnest. To his further amazement, whenever someone in another car glanced in His direction, the Voice would simply fade to "liquid glass," then back to substance when they looked away.

"What do you want out of your business life?" The Voice asked with a passion that reminded Jim of how he, himself, once felt. "What is your purpose in your career? What do you want to accomplish in your lifetime? What would you do if money was not an issue?"

"Wow," Jim shifted his grip on the wheel from the 10/2 position to 8/4, trying to relax. "That's a lot to think about—I feel like my head's going to explode."

"Fine, Jim, just take the first question."

"What do I want out of my business life? Well, let's see…" Jim rubbed his chin with his right hand, steadying the wheel with his other. "Well, like everyone else, I guess I want to work till I am sixty or sixty-five, save a lot of money and retire in a nice warm place with my wife. I don't know, what does anyone want in life?

"Is this a trick question?" Jim blurted out, then immediately regretted it.

"Not at all." The Voice seemed to be slightly amused. "Let's say it's thirty years from now and you are sixty-seven. With what you just told me, what would you have accomplished in your life? What would you have spent your entire work life doing? What would you have left behind? Think carefully about it."

"I don't know how to answer you," Jim said, tightening his grip on the wheel and biting his lip.

"Your purpose is a route that you chart out for yourself in your career." The Voice was firm, yet soothing and supportive. "It is not short term, but continuous. It is not about making money unless that money is to benefit others. You have to align what you believe in with the way you do business. Every person on this earth has a purpose, but you need to listen to your inner voice and be truthful with yourself to determine what it is. Everyone is here to make the world a better place in some large or small way. You were not put on this earth to work for forty years and merely survive and leave nothing behind. There is something that you are pretending is not there. Until you declare your purpose you will never feel true fulfillment."

Jim shook his head in frustration and hunched forward, the color draining from his face. "But I don't know where to start."

"That's because you are making it too hard. It doesn't have to be complicated," the Voice smiled and with that small gesture Jim found himself relaxing his grip on the wheel and sitting back. "To some it is helping the sick, feeding the poor, or educating young minds. To others it is leading by example for those who work around them, or using the talents they have learned or contacts they have made to help others. It could be manufacturing a product that benefits society. But without a higher purpose, work is empty. Live as the person you know deep down inside that you really are. What is your deepest desire? What have you always dreamed of? What have you always wanted to do? Declare who you are! Be who you are. Business is what you make of it. Be a pilot, not just a passenger."

Jim sat up straighter and his color came back. It felt like the blood that was coursing through his veins had picked up speed. Ideas that a few seconds ago seemed miles away were now rushing at him like the oncoming freeway traffic. "I want to help others. And I *can* help others. I want to give something back. I know as much about real estate as anyone I know, and I'm sure there are lots of people who could use my help." Jim realized his travel mug of coffee had been untouched and would probably be too cold for his liking by now. The traffic had opened up to a 45 mph pace and as he reached for the mug to test the temperature, he was suddenly cut off by an inconsiderate driver and had to quickly apply his brakes. But instead of hammering his horn as usual, Jim made a 'be my guest' gesture.

"There are charitable organizations looking for a head-quarters, groups looking for donations of merchandise or food that many of my clients may have an excess of in their warehouses, and would benefit from a charitable deduction. Come to think of it, there is a lot of good to be done out there. I have an idea of how I might get started within my current job, and maybe this can lead to a whole new business of my own that can even make a profit for me to support my family, but also greatly benefit many others. This is great! This is exciting! Thanks!"

Jim was practically bouncing in his seat as a police car pulled alongside on the right and paced him. The cop looked right through the Voice at Jim, trying to decipher if he was high on something. Jim noticed he was being watched by a patrolman and began to pretend he was be-bopping to a song on the radio. Then abruptly, he sat up straight and took on a somber expression to indicate, 'see, I'm cool.' The policeman was satisfied and moved on.

The Voice appeared to be amused by Jim's tactic.

"Anyway, thanks, really! I mean it!" Jim gushed.

"I did nothing Jim. All of that has been inside of you for some time. All I did was help you listen to your inner voice." The Voice motioned to the upcoming exit; otherwise Jim would have driven right past it. Jim had to merge fast across three crowded lanes, but he successfully executed the maneuver as cars were suddenly, and improbably, slowing down to help him make it onto the exit ramp.

"The important thing is that you must now take responsibility for stating your purpose and changing your life." Jim had reached the bottom of the ramp and was turning right as the Voice continued. "You don't have to know all of the answers now. That is not important. In due time everything will become more clear to you if you continue to listen. As the old saying goes, 'Let Go and Let God.' You have the power to change your life and to make it what you want it to be. Taking responsibility is the first step!"

"Oh darn, here we are at work already." Jim pointed to a large building just up ahead. He couldn't believe how fast the time had flown. Lately the drive to work felt like hours were elapsing. But today it seemed to have happened in a blink. He turned into the company parking lot and pulled into his assigned space. "That was the fastest trip that I can remember. You've given me a lot to think about."

Jim was hesitant to ask the question that was pressing on his mind. Sensing this, the Voice inquired, "Yes, Jim? Go ahead and ask."

"Um…" his voice cracked as he said uneasily, "can we talk again?"

"Any time you want to, Jim."

Jim let loose a sigh of relief.

"All you have to do is ask and I will be there for you. But as you said, you have a lot to think about today. Why don't

27

we meet again tomorrow morning and talk some more? We can carpool to work again tomorrow, if you'd like."

"If I'd like?" Jim practically exploded. "You kidding? What kind of a fool would I be to turn down an offer like that?"

Jim made a 'sorry' gesture with his hand, acknowledging he was perhaps out of line with that last remark. "I mean, I will be looking forward to it."

The Voice simply flashed a mesmerizing smile. To Jim's dumbfounded amazement, the smile just got wider and wider until all that formerly appeared to be flesh and fabric folded into it. And then He was gone.

Jim got out of his car, popped the trunk and grabbed his briefcase. He went into work with a hop in his step and a big smile on his face.

"And now I will show you the most excellent way."
1 Corinthians 12:31

Chapter Two - INTEGRITY

"There is no right way to do a wrong thing.."
- Kenneth Blanchard and Norman Vincent Peale

"Ability will enable a man to go to the top, but it takes character to keep him there." - God's Little Instruction Book

Jim was full of excitement the entire day and couldn't wait until the next morning for his ride to work. He was daydreaming about the future and jotting down notes. Jim decided it would be best if he told absolutely no one about his new carpool Companion, lest they think him crazy or the very least, that he was starting to lose it. After a prayer of thanks for all of the blessings in his life, and a promise to himself to make prayer a daily practice, he went to bed that night with his mind racing and a smile on his face. He reflected on the past 15 years of his career and how he as a person had changed—from the innocent idealistic dreamer to a much more practical "do what needs to be done" type of executive. He had changed a lot more than he had realized. Suddenly the smile was replaced by a look of concern as he dozed off into a night of restless sleep.

The next morning, Jim went through his normal ritual, pouring his cup of coffee, grabbing his briefcase and then off to the garage. He got into his car and backed out onto the street. He began to worry if perhaps it had all been a hallucination—what if the Voice would not be there?

The passenger seat was empty. Instinctually, he turned his head upward to the heavens and said hello. He waited a couple of seconds and repeated it. Nothing. He began to concentrate on his driving and said out loud, "I really hope that everything that happened to me yesterday wasn't just my imagination. This is the best I have felt about my life in a long time. Please come join me."

"Hello," came the familiar, gentle Voice as He materialized in the passenger seat. He was dressed the same as before, but this time Jim noticed that His complexion seemed to glow. He did not look around, but focused His attention and energy on Jim. And yet, He seemed to be *taking in*, or was *aware*, of everything, 360 degrees, at all times.

"Hello!" Jim's face registered relief and excitement that his new Friend was back. He was anxious to share his thoughts of the day before. But within moments, a troubled look crossed Jim's face.

"You looked very happy when you left Me yesterday, but you don't now," the Voice observed.

Jim raked the fingers of his right hand through his hair. It was something he often did when he was frustrated. "Yes, I was very happy yesterday and in fact I am still excited about working out the new purpose in my life, but all of this thinking has opened up many other issues for me and I really didn't sleep very well because of it."

"Tell me more," the Voice encouraged.

Jim stiffened both arms against the wheel, pushed his head back against the headrest, and shifted in his seat. "Fifteen years ago, when I came to the company right out of college, I was idealistic and headstrong. I'd been raised to do things the right way. I never really stopped to think about how much I have changed and how much of my idealism has been compromised. The simple lies to close a deal, the fudging of numbers to make the quarter, the occasional back-stabbing of others, false promises, breaking my word, all seemingly innocent, but fifteen years worth of small chinks in my armor all add up."

Jim saw the crosswalk up ahead and immediately slowed down. But the crossing guard didn't have a queue of kids this time, so he picked up a little speed. "I can still clearly visualize one big burly vice-president with a British accent saying, 'don't be so naïve Jim, everyone lies in this business.

31

That's how it's done.' I will never forget his face. It wasn't until later that I found out he had a history of questionable business practices that bordered on criminal. I slowly got in line and did all the right things for the company to make its numbers, but I now realize that I have compromised myself in the process."

"You can start all over today," the Voice said calmly. "Do you know that?"

Jim could only stare back in disbelief.

"You can revitalize your integrity and start to only do things the right way. That's the beauty of it—it's never too late to start. In your heart you always know what is right and what is wrong."

"You know, it's funny," Jim mused, "this past weekend we rented a movie called *Spy Kids Two* that the whole family watched. The lead girl character was talking to her archrival about doing the right thing. The other girl asked her how you know what is right. The lead girl looked at her and said 'when the time comes, you will know.' Such simple words spoken in a children's movie now hit me right between the eyes. I guess that I have always known, but have conveniently convinced myself that it is okay to cut corners in business."

"It's been said that the real test of your integrity is what you do when no one else is looking."

Jim suddenly realized he was in the wrong lane for his freeway onramp. But almost miraculously, the cars on his right slowed down as soon as he hit his turn signal to let him cut in front of them.

The Voice continued, "You must be able to look at yourself in the mirror each morning and see yourself as you really are. When you can do that and be proud of what you see, then you are living your life with integrity. You have to trust your inner voice and determine how you feel about what you are doing. Ultimately you become what you do every day. If your actions are dishonest, you become a dishonest person. People are known by the way they act and that becomes their reputation and the legacy that they carry with them. Being a person of integrity means that you act that way *all* the time, not just when it is the convenient thing to do."

Jim accelerated up the onramp. "As Shakespeare reportedly said, 'No legacy is as rich as honesty.'"

"And as I reportedly said," the Voice returned, "'A good name is more desirable than great riches; to be esteemed is better than silver or gold' — Proverbs Twenty-two, Verse one."

The Voice's show of humor put Jim more at ease with himself.

"Don't ever sacrifice your name and reputation. It is the only one you have and it is very difficult to get it back. You must be the judge as to whether or not your actions are those of a person of integrity."

"This is too bizarre," Jim chuckled, "I had a fortune cookie at lunch the other day that read, 'Judge yourself by your actions, and others by their intentions, and you will always be happy.'"

"What's so bizarre?" the Voice smiled knowingly, "Didn't I tell you yesterday that I'm always communicating with you in many ways?"

Jim could only shake his head in wonderment.

"Jim, you will not have any trouble sleeping when you confidently know that all of your actions are those of a person of integrity. Always tell the truth. Always keep your word. Lead by example and live by *your* principles, not those of others. There is often an immediate price to pay, but the cost of doing things the wrong way will always be much greater in the end."

"I guess it was my conscience that kept me up last night."

"Deep down inside you always know whether or not you are living your life as an honest and truthful person. Your inner voice knows what is right and what is wrong and you can only hide from it for so long. That truth burns inside of you like a bright light and the more times that you do something dishonest, the dimmer that light becomes."

Jim picked up speed to merge over two lanes and catch the exit ramp before it passed him by. "It feels like it is time for my light to burn bright once again."

"Jim, you realize that you will be tested," the Voice cautioned him. "Although your inner voice will always tell you what is right and what is wrong it won't always be easy for you to listen. What if going in a dishonest direction pays you much more money? What if being honest causes you to lose an important contract? What if the truth causes you to miss your quarterly quota? What will you do then? How will you respond?"

"There's always a catch, isn't there?" Jim frowned. "I guess that I won't really know until the next time I am challenged. I certainly will commit myself to doing the right thing each and every time. But what if I make mistakes?"

"Simple," the Voice assured him, "Acknowledge those mistakes. Take responsibility for them and don't make excuses, or try to pass the blame onto someone else."

"Should I ask for Your forgiveness?"

"If it will make you feel better," the Voice grinned. "But more important is that you pick yourself up, dust yourself off, and start anew. Keep listening to your inner voice and do your utmost to live as a person of integrity. "

Misjudging his speed, Jim had to brake hard at the bottom of the off-ramp. "This is not going to be easy."

"You are very wise Jim, much wiser than even you realize. I am very happy for you now. You are ready for so much more."

Jim entered the company parking lot feeling somewhat overwhelmed by the task ahead of him. He took a deep breath and daringly asked, "When can we meet again?"

"When would you like to meet again?"

Jim overshot his assigned parking space. "This is almost too good to be true. I can really meet with you any time that I want?"

"Don't be so surprised," the Voice said serenely, "that's always been your choice to make."

Jim backed up a few feet and pulled into his space. "You know, when I first started working, over my lunch hour I would often go to this beautiful little park just down the street. It has a pond surrounded by benches where you can sit, eat and unwind. I could always go off and think in peace and quiet and reflect on what was going on in my life. I haven't done that in years."

"Sounds nice. I will see you there tomorrow at…"

"Uh," Jim said, picking up his cue, "is twelve-thirty okay?"

"I'll see you there tomorrow at twelve-thirty."

"Again, I have an awful lot to think about today."

"I look forward to tomorrow. Peace be with you today Jim." The Voice slowly closed His eyes, dematerializing simultaneously.

Jim got out of the car, popped the trunk and grabbed his briefcase. He quick-stepped to his office.

"I have chosen the way of truth." Psalms 119:30

"…the truth will set you free." John 8:32

Chapter Three - COMMITMENT

"The quality of a person's life is in direct proportion to their commitment to excellence, regardless of their chosen field of endeavor." - Vincent T. Lombardi

"…any road to achieving one's maximum potential must be built on a bedrock of respect for the individual, a commitment to excellence, and a rejection of mediocrity." - Buck Rodgers

The next day, Jim left the office at noon and stopped at a local deli to buy a sandwich and soda, and walked at a fast clip to the park. The park was almost empty as he found a bench facing the pond. He sat down and started to eat his lunch. As he turned around he realized that he had Company on the bench.

"Good afternoon, Jim," said the Voice, gesturing broadly. "This is a beautiful place. You should come here more often."

"You're right," Jim confessed, "I should come here more often to clear my head and think. I used to come here a lot. I don't know why I stopped."

Jim held up his sandwich and shrugged, "I almost bought one for you, but then I figured..."

The Voice just smiled.

"You said that you had lost your way in life and this is just one more aspect of that." The Voice beckoned Jim to continue eating.

"What do you mean?" Jim asked before taking a bite.

"You are lacking commitment, Jim."

"But I love my wife," Jim protested. "I try to do right by her..."

"Not commitment in your marriage or to your family," The Voice corrected him, "but to yourself. You are not committed to yourself."

"I don't understand?" Jim's expression clouded as he took a sip of his soda, "I worked long and hard for many years for the company, sometimes putting in fifty to sixty hours per week."

"You aren't doing that anymore, are you?" the Voice replied in a tone completely free of accusation. "But I am not just talking about working long hours and doing the best you can. To go the extra yard is certainly a big part of being successful in life, however, what I am really talking about is a commitment to your *self*. A commitment to someone or something else is important, but the commitment you make to attain your purpose in life is the most important commitment you will ever make."

"Oh my gosh. You are right." Jim put down his sandwich and soft drink in order to focus his full attention on their conversation. "But, where do I start?" Overwhelmed, he threw up his hands.

"Well, that's actually up to you," the Voice said kindly. "If you want to accomplish great things you need to make a great commitment. You first need to rekindle your commitment to your current job, and then begin to plot your course to achieve your purpose. Only you can determine your route and your timetable. The important thing is to be committed to the end result, your purpose."

"But I'm not totally clear yet on my purpose. Can you tell me what it is—or at least give me a hint?"

The Voice smiled at this. "There is no clear direction for you to take and your path will likely be fraught with frustration and distractions. Still, you must persevere."

"But how?" Jim threw his arms open in a pleading gesture. In doing so, he knocked over his soda, but he made a grab and caught it at the last second before it hit the ground. Jim glanced up at the Voice, wondering if He had a Hand in the "lucky" catch. But the Voice gave no indication. Finally, Jim asked, "What should I do to discover my purpose?"

"As I said before, listen to your inner voice. It is talking to you all the time—just like I am now—trying to get a message to you. That is your *hint.*"

Jim became reflective. "You know, I recently watched a movie on TV called *The Legend of Bagger Vance*. Will Smith and Matt Damon are the lead characters. Will Smith plays a caddy who was hired to help rejuvenate Matt Damon's career as a professional golfer. Smith offered several insights, but the most meaningful lesson that he taught Damon was that he needed to drown out everything else around him and to focus only on the flag in the hole. And once he did that, the shots he needed to take would be made very clear to him, and would almost be calling to him. Anyway, it worked and Matt Damon made a big comeback to tie with the two other competitors—it was a 'win-win-win' situation."

The Voice's eyes turned upward. "Good analogy, Jim. Your purpose in life is like the flag way off on the green. It may take you a lot of strokes to get there, but you have to keep focusing on it and keep playing the game. You have to stay committed."

"But, how do I start?" Jim pleaded. "Can you at least tell me that?"

"Start by writing down your purpose—or what you think your purpose is—on a piece of paper. Just make sure it has something to do with giving back, or somehow helping others. Your purpose is not really about *you*. It's about how you are going to contribute to the betterment of mankind. It is about the legacy that you will leave behind when you are no longer on this planet." By turning His eyes ever so slightly, the Voice Himself appeared to turn directly toward Jim. "Then write down any thoughts you might now have about how you will work toward your purpose. And remember, your purpose is like the flag in your movie metaphor that is out in front of you, that you are trying to reach. Writing things down will help to have everything make sense. As you think about it and visualize the flag, remember that your inner voice will guide you to it. Always listen to your inner voice. Find quiet times and places like this one to clear your mind and to think. Don't be frustrated if everything is not clear to you, for all of your answers will come. It is all part of the process. You have been blessed with all of the tools that you need to lead a wonderful and fulfilling life. All you need to do is use them. So, feel good about yourself and listen to yourself."

"I believe I understand," said Jim. "I think I need to spend more quiet time with no TV or other distractions. I really ought to come here on a more regular basis."

"How are you feeling right now?" The Voice asked.

"The task you have laid out for me feels a little overwhelming, but I am really excited for the first time in a long time. Thanks. I'd better be getting back to work." Jim gathered up the remnants of his lunch and put them into the paper bag. He began crumpling it into the shape of a ball, and took note of a nearby trashcan.

"I am glad that I could help, Jim."

Jim got up and turned to face the Voice. "When can we meet again?"

"Would you like to meet me at work tomorrow?" the Voice asked nonchalantly.

Jim almost dropped his crumpled bag. "Can you do that? Will everyone else be able to see and hear You?"

"I will be there for you and you alone Jim. I would love to go to your office with you tomorrow," the Voice glimmered. "I will see you then. Goodbye."

Jim said goodbye, and headed back to his office. About ten feet from the trashcan, he executed a jump shot and launched the bag in a perfect arc. Swish!

"Nothin' but net!" he laughed.

"Whatever you do, work at it with all your heart."

Colossians 3:23

Chapter Four - THE COURAGE OF CONVICTION

"Only those who dare to fail greatly ever achieve greatly." - Robert F. Kennedy

"Nice guys may appear to finish last, but usually they're running in a different race." - Ken Blanchard and Norman Vincent Peale

Jim's mind churned all that night. He was filled with excitement the next morning when he left for work. He pulled into his parking space, got out of his car and walked toward his building. As he reached to open the front door, he heard a familiar Voice from behind him ask, "How are you today Jim?"

Jim spun around and quickly looked in all directions to make sure no one else was present, then replied, "Great thanks, I am very excited today. Let's go up to my office."

As they walked side-by-side into the building, the Voice first turned fuzzy around His edges, like a camera shot that is out of focus. A moment later, He was invisible, an Energy force that Jim could sense but not see.

Jim and the Voice rode the elevator up to the 4th Floor where his office was. Jim quickly ducked into the empty break room to grab a cup of coffee. As he made his way to his office, he could sense the Energy force of the Voice matching his stride beside him. Jim had a sense that others were looking at him funny as he nodded a few quick hellos. He couldn't tell if some of his coworkers were sensing a Presence beside him, or if it was just his imagination that their gazes seemed to remain fixed on him after their louder-than-usual return hellos.

Jim entered his office, closed the door, and sat in his desk chair. The Voice took one of the chairs facing Jim's desk and rematerialized.

Realizing his desk was a little messy and cluttered with paperwork, Jim set his cup of coffee down and began to straighten up, making a couple of neat piles. "You know, I am really excited right now. My mind just continues to race with new ideas. The unfortunate thing is that now reality sets back in."

"How so, Jim?" the Voice inquired.

"I have to go to our weekly management review meeting in twenty minutes, during which I will be expected to act in the same compromising fashion that everyone else does, and that I have gradually acquiesced to, myself. My integrity will indeed be challenged," Jim said, putting the finishing touches on his desktop organization. "How do I deal with that?"

"Facing adversity is a simple fact of life," the Voice explained. "Everyone is tested. Circumstances will always arise in which an easier route will appear that may compromise your integrity. In most cases, this easier option will provide greater short-term rewards than taking the route of integrity. That is when people really prove what they are made of. You may suffer some discomfort initially, but you will definitely benefit in the long run."

"So what do you suggest? What would You do if You were in my shoes?" Jim asked, looking down and making a face, "besides *shine* them?"

The Voice smiled at Jim's impromptu humor. "The best way to deal with any issue is head on. Will you have the courage of conviction to stand up for yourself and what you believe in? Will you stand tall and face your adversary? When things aren't working for you, what will you do?"

Jim pondered this as he picked up a paperweight and began tossing it from one hand to the other. "You make it sound so simple. But it is not simple to swim against the tide. It is not simple to tell your boss that you don't intend to do something his way, especially when there is someone else who is always willing to do what you refuse to. And that someone wants your job. It is just not simple at all."

"You're right Jim, it is not easy," the Voice acknowledged. "It takes great courage to listen to your inner voice and to stand up for what you believe in, particularly when your actions may seem very foolish to others—or perhaps put your career at risk. Many times you have to move forward simply based on faith, on knowing that your inner voice is telling you what is right. Trust your instincts, Jim. The choice is always yours."

Jim exchanged the paperweight for a ballpoint pen and began slowly clicking it open and closed. "I have to admit that I am somewhat frightened by this. It is never easy to buck your peers, or cross the guy who signs your paycheck."

"The promise that I will make to you is that I will always be by your side, whether you know it or not, or whether you ask Me to be there or not," the Voice said, His eyes reassuring. "I will always be there to pick you up no matter how many times you might be knocked down. If you allow Me to I will help to guide your every step. Hopefully, knowing that I am always there will help soothe your fear. Always listen to your inner voice. That is how you will hear my guidance."

"There's that *inner voice* again," Jim chimed, shaking his head. "I guess that I will never be able to ignore it again!"

The Voice became more urgent. "I really can't say it enough. It is everyone's direct connection to Me. But even knowing that, most people will fail to use it."

"I have to read you an e-mail that a friend of mine from church sent me the other day." Jim quickly pecked a couple of keys on his computer keyboard then scrolled down with his mouse. "Ah, here it is." He right-clicked and a Window opened. "It's called, 'Memo from God.' I wish I knew who the author was."

"Well, I can tell you Who was the inspiration for it." The Voice flashed a smile.

Jim raised his eyebrows and grinned at the Voice's comment before turning his attention to his computer screen. "It reads, 'Should you find yourself a victim of other people's bitterness, ignorance, smallness or insecurities—remember things could be worse. You could be them!'"

"And the moral of the memo is?" the Voice prompted.

"I guess instead of worrying so much about what others think or say, that I should simply be thankful that You are there to guide me—and that I no longer block my inner voice the way they do. I feel blessed."

"Then why the tension lines in your forehead?" the Voice observed.

"The question I have now is," Jim self-consciously put his hand to his forehead, trying to rub them out, "what if I can't do things the right way and still survive in this job?

What do I do if they just keep tightening the screws? What happens if they stop promoting me, or worse, fire me?"

"Jim, hopefully that will never happen," the Voice said, His expression turning serious. "You would be surprised how many times that people back off when faced with the way of integrity. Although they might do their best to block out their inner voice, when confronted with issues of integrity their inner voice will yell as loud as it can to be heard. It is sort of like looking in the mirror at yourself and seeing the real you—if only for a brief moment."

Jim nodded acknowledgement as he looked at a timeline on his desk calendar then glanced at his watch. He picked up a tension ball and began to squeeze it—fast at first, but slower and more effortlessly as the soothing Voice continued.

"Being true to your values is much more important to your life than any short term setback. You can always get a better job or another promotion. You only have one soul and you can never give that away. Sometimes you may just need to walk away, even if it causes you some short-term pain, discomfort or inconvenience. Most people will respect you more for taking a stand, at least all the people who are really important to you. I assure you that if you and I agree on an issue, then the benefits of your virtue will be plainly evident to you during your lifetime. The key is that you must meet your problems head on and quickly deal with adversity."

Jim's secretary buzzed him on the intercom to let him know that the weekly budget review meeting was about to start. Jim turned to the Voice and said, "I have to go. But I feel we're not quite finished with this conversation yet. Can we meet later?"

"Where and when?"

"Will you meet me in my den at home tonight?"

"I'll be there, Jim. Remember, even though you won't see me, I will be right by your side all day long." The Voice's countenance brightened and appeared to envelop Jim before disappearing altogether.

"God is our refuge and strength, an ever present help in trouble."

Psalm 46:1

"I can do everything through God who gives me strength."

Philippians 4:13

Chapter Five - ENERGY AND ENTHUSIASM

"Nothing great was ever achieved without enthu-siasm." - Ralph Waldo Emerson

"Enthusiasm is the greatest asset in the world. It beats money, power and influence." - Henry Chester

Jim came home from work that night, tired after his long day, had dinner with his family and then spent some time with his children. After he and his wife had gotten the children to bed, Jim told his wife that he needed to spend some time in the den to do a little preparation for the next day. For many years, Jim had made it a habit to go into his den in the late evening hours to plan his next day and spend some time thinking about what was going on at work. He would jot down notes, read articles and books about business management and then would start the next day filled with excitement, using his notes from the night before as inspiration. In recent years, many of his evenings had been spent curled up on the couch, watching a movie on cable, or one of his favorite sports teams play. He made little or no preparation for the following day anymore. Now, Jim usually waited to get to work to see what happened. He handled things as they came up and did whatever planning for his direct reports as was necessary. In a pinch, he sometimes worked late, but clearly his enthusiasm for his work had all but disappeared. Tonight he was inspired to spend some time alone, trying to sort out everything that was going on in his life right now. He felt like his whole life had been turned on end and he wasn't really sure what to do about it. In his heart he knew that he had started back on the right path. He sat down at his desk and turned on his computer.

"Good evening Jim," came the comforting Voice from an overstuffed chair on the other side of Jim's desk. "How are you tonight?"

Jim looked up and broke into a wide smile. "Boy, am I glad to see you."

"Likewise."

"This has been an amazing week!" Jim said, leaning back in his chair. "I feel like You have just reached inside of me and have shaken everything up. Last week I was telling myself that I had everything I could expect out of life, even though I really didn't believe it deep down inside. Today I am more excited than I have been in many years and people really responded to it.

"I take it you're talking about your meeting this afternoon."

"Did you see their faces?" Jim said, leaning forward. "What am I saying? Of course You did. I could feel Your presence.

"It was so cool, watching people brighten up as I spoke. I felt very powerful. And now I feel like this light has come on inside of me."

"Jim," the Voice smiled warmly, "that light is your enthusiasm for your work turning on again after a long period of darkness."

Jim clenched his fist in acknowledgement.

"Enthusiasm is a critical ingredient of success. People responded to you today because you made your enthusiasm fill the room that you were in. You stimulated others and they reacted in a very positive way. People love to be inspired by others. Those people face all the same challenges and disappointments as you do and are subject to the same highs and lows that you are."

Jim was happily nodding his head like a bobble doll.

"When you share your enthusiasm with others they will listen to you, and follow you, and most significantly, be inspired by you. You can solicit their support to overcome whatever obstacles get in your way."

"Yes," Jim pumped his fist, "I now know exactly what you mean."

"Use your enthusiasm as your own personal catalyst. Enthusiasm and excitement add importance to everything that you do in life. It shows others that you are confident in what you believe in, and it raises their confidence and morale as well. Enthusiasm is a very valuable thing! You can do everything with it, but very little without it."

Jim thought for a second and said, "You nailed it once again! History is filled with examples of leaders whose enthusiasm inspired others and helped them to accomplish amazing feats and overcome huge obstacles."

"We tend to think about famous biblical figures, historical heroes, politicians or generals as those that inspire others, but enthusiasm and excitement are incredible tools for anyone."

"This may sound very odd to you..." Jim offered.

"Try me," the Voice urged him on.

"A real-life example of how one person's enthusiasm served as a catalyst, happened a few years ago in the NBA. A guard named Jason Kidd was traded to the lowly New Jersey Nets, a perpetual doormat during their twenty-five years in the league. At the press conference held to announce his arrival, he proclaimed, 'We're going to turn this team around three-hundred-sixty degrees.' Everyone laughed at this. He went on to tell the reporters that this team that had won only twenty-six games the year before, and had the same coach, and almost all of the same players, would win forty games or more. The reporters laughed even louder. In pre-season practice, Jason filled the training camp with excitement by constantly displaying his unbridled enthusiasm. The team started playing well from the very start of the season and played hard throughout. The result—they doubled their total of wins from the prior year and won the Eastern Conference title. Kidd inspired millions of people all over the world."

"Enthusiasm makes everyone's world better, whether it is the crossing guard, a grocery clerk, a teacher, an astronaut or an athlete," said the Voice. "Be positive and positive things happen around you! Wake up each day truly believing that this is going to be a great day! Live each day like it is going to be your last. Welcome each day wondering what wonderful thing is going to happen. You will shine like a light to all around you and brighten everyone's day as well as yours. Don't hold back. Keep that light turned on brightly."

Jim was swiveling left then right in his chair, barely able to contain his excitement.

"Jim, you will see the impact that you have on everyone you work with, especially those who work for you and look to you as a role model. You will help to make their lives better and the world a little bit brighter."

"I will be that light!" Jim vowed. "For others and for myself. I want everyone to see how wonderful it is to have You as a partner. I feel better right now than I have for a long, long time. This week I truly am the luckiest man on earth!"

"That you are Jim." The Voice held up an open palm. "But not just this week. You've always been very fortunate—you just weren't always aware of it."

"When can we meet again?" Jim was boiling over with emotion. "Will you ride to work with me tomorrow?"

"I will see you tomorrow morning, Jim."

"Shout aloud and sing for joy..."
Isaiah 12:16

Chapter Six - RESPECT

"Condemn the fault and not the actor of it."
- Shakespeare

"People who look down on other people
don't end up being looked up to." - Robert Half

Jim went through his normal ritual the next morning, pouring his cup of coffee into his travel mug, saying goodbye to his wife and kids, and then went off to his car. He backed out of the garage and into the street and started his drive to work.

"It's a beautiful day, Jim," the Voice said as He became visible. "The sun is shining and the spring flowers are in bloom. But you look very serious. What is on your mind?"

"I am troubled," Jim answered, shaking his head. "I am now committed to doing the right thing in everything I do. Yes, I can be responsible for myself and those who work for me, but how do I respect a boss who does not do things with integrity?"

"Tell me more."

"Yesterday I found out that in an effort to close a big deal that we have been working on, my boss told a customer an out-and-out lie." Jim slowed down and looked both ways before proceeding through the school crossing. "He promised them that a deal had already been signed to build a McDonald's on one side of this property and a Wal-Mart on the other side of it."

"And you know this is not true," the Voice said with certainty.

"No it's not." Jim picked up a little speed. "He then told them that he didn't want them to be left out because the price of this property was certain to go up a lot in the very near future, which is another lie. I can't control his actions. How do I treat him with respect?"

"Respect is a very complex issue," the Voice explained. "One part of it is what you have brought up. You don't have to respect a person who happens to be your boss, but you do have to respect their position. It is very clearly written in the Bible that you must respect authority. You do not have to approve of what they do, and you certainly must not act the way they do, but as long as they are your bosses, there is a level of respect that must be given to them. You can choose to discuss the situation with them and try to show them the right way. If they are doing something that is illegal or against company codes, you can choose to report them to their superiors or your personnel department. If they own the company and haven't broken any laws, and you cannot influence them to change, then you must learn to live with what they are doing without compromising your own integrity, or choose to leave and get another job. It is difficult enough to work for someone whom you don't like, but do respect; working for someone you don't respect is much more difficult, whether you like them or not."

"I guess that I am the only one who can decide how to deal with my present situation." Jim accelerated up the freeway ramp. "I will have to give it a lot of thought. As long as no one tries to force me to compromise my own integrity, I guess I can deal with it. I have been at Foremost my whole career. I could not simply walk out. I must try to make it work until I have a clearer definition of how I will fulfill my purpose in life."

"Listen to your inner voice."

Jim nodded affirmatively upon hearing that familiar line.

"Do what you know is right. Never compromise on who you are."

"You said that this is one part of respect," Jim said as he glanced at his rearview mirror then merged. "Is there something else I should be concerned about?"

"Another part is the respect that you give to others, and earning the respect of others," the Voice replied. "Respecting others is a way that you earn the respect of others. You must give respect to get respect. No matter what job you have, or how much money you have, no one on this earth is better than any other one. Every one of you was created as an equal. It is something that you must remind yourself each and every day. Everyone is someone's son or daughter. Most people are someone's brother, sister, cousin or friend. They were born like you were and will some day die just like you will."

"You had to remind me of that?" Jim winced as he crossed over into the fast lane.

The Voice smiled graciously. "There is something special about everyone on Earth. Treat everyone you meet with respect. Speak with respect and acknowledge those people you come in contact with. Say 'please' and 'thank you' and give credit where credit is due."

"That's not always easy, but I see your point."

"It has been said that the way you treat others is the real opinion that you have of yourself."

"That's good," Jim grinned, "I like that."

"Learn to lead people and not to use them. Learn to trust people and they will pay you dividends back in return. Give people the benefit of the doubt. And I know it's hard, but try your best not to be judgmental."

Jim noticed his exit ramp was coming up soon. "I used to have a saying taped to my computer. It said, 'you meet the same people on the way down as you do on the way up.'

"That's good," the Voice sparkled, "I like that."

Jim laughed with careless abandon. "Even though I am usually pleasant to others, I have been a little full of myself recently. I certainly could treat people with more respect and work harder to earn their respect."

"Think about what a world filled with respect looks like, Jim," the Voice said with wonderment. "Your fellow employees will be happier and you will be happier. Everyone will be more satisfied and therefore more productive. There will be no gossip, no politics and no backstabbing. Everyone is working toward a common goal, fully supportive of the efforts of all around him or her."

"If only that could be..."

"There is another part of respect," the Voice declared.

"What's that?"

"Self respect," the Voice emphasized, "you need to feel good about who you are and what you do. When you respect yourself you build your self-esteem. Choose to feel good about yourself. Believe that you are capable of big things and you will accomplish them. Imagine your dream and then make it happen."

"Suddenly Aretha Franklin's voice is filling my head." Jim began tapping his steering wheel and singing. "R-E-S-P-E-C-T. Find out what it means to me. R-E-S-P-E-C-T..." Jim glanced over and noticed that the Voice had turned transparent. Directly to his right, a bunch of kids in the back of a mini-van were pointing at him and giggling. He blushed, then quickly composed himself and picked up speed, leaving the van behind. "Sorry, I couldn't help it. But I get what you mean. I have to respect authority, I have to respect others and I have to respect myself. I am not better than anyone and no one is better than me, and we must all treat each other with common courtesy and respect."

"And what else?" the Voice inquired as He reappeared.

"I must first treat others with respect, and in turn I will receive their respect. I must have respect for my talents and believe in myself. Respect is like a bridge—it takes a long time to build, and may appear to be very sturdy. But if sabotaged, it could come crashing down in a moment."

Jim made his way down the exit ramp. "I feel like I'm really making progress, but tomorrow is Saturday and I don't want to stop. Is there any way we can meet tomorrow?"

"Of course, Jim," the Voice appeared to nod. "Where would you like to meet?"

"I'm going to take an early morning bike ride tomorrow—like I used to every Saturday. Can we can meet in Morris Park at the far end of the bike path where I always stop for a break?"

"I will be there," the Voice assured Jim as He faded from view.

"Do to others as you would have them do to you."
Luke 6:31

Chapter Seven - HUMILITY

"A man wrapped up inside of himself makes a very small package." - God's Little Instruction Book

"We have to acquire a peace and balance of mind such that we can give every word of criticism its due weight, and humble ourselves before every word of praise." - Dag Hammarskjold

Jim got up early on Saturday and rode his bike from his home to the bike trail at Morris Park. He rode to the far end of the park, and was now approximately eight miles from his home. He stopped to fill his water bottle and rest on a park bench. Jim used to take this ride very frequently, but lately he was lucky to do it once every two months. The ride was peaceful and beautiful, winding through the woods and out to a clearing at the far end where he now sat. It was a great place to think.

Jim was a little out of breath and somewhat parched. He took a drink from his water bottle, then got up and walked over to his bike, resting on its kickstand a few feet away.

"Good morning, Jim," came the Voice as He materialized on the park bench Jim had just vacated.

"Isn't it beautiful here?" Jim motioned left and right with one hand as he put his water bottle back in its holder on the bike frame. "I really love this ride."

"Yes, it certainly is." The Voice appeared to be taking in the entire park, yet His gaze remained fixed on Jim. "The best thing about it is that it's very humbling."

"Why do you say that?" Jim asked, giving Him an odd look.

"Out here, any person is forced to realize how they are just one small ingredient of the near perfect world that was created for you," the Voice said, gesturing wide and far. "In your world of business, people tend to give themselves a certain amount of added importance because of how much money they make or what job they have."

"I could rattle off about ten senior executives I know who fit that category."

Jim leaned slightly over his bike, resting one arm on his seat.

"One must never let pride transform into unbridled vanity," the Voice cautioned. "When someone thinks they know everything they stop listening and stop learning, and as a result, they stop growing as a person. Their wealth might grow, but spiritually they become dormant. When you lose your humility and think that you know everything, you tend to no longer be aware of what is really going on around you."

"That's like the story of *The Emperor's New Clothes*, isn't it?" Jim straightened up and shifted his weight to his heels. "He thought that he looked so wonderful, but he was really just standing there in his underwear."

"Good analogy, Jim." The Voice looked amused.

"Being humble and continuing to listen to others, and being really aware of what is happening around you is a real challenge," Jim continued. "It is much easier to feel better than someone who doesn't have a job or a house as good as yours. And it's easier to close your ears to what other people are saying and try to dominate conversations—only really caring about what you have to say. I guess that I have been guilty of that a few times."

The Voice beamed. "I'm glad that you are opening your eyes to certain things. Pride and an over-inflated ego can get in a person's way."

Jim absently began squeezing the brake lever with one hand. "I recently read a real estate trade journal in which a gentleman that I used to work with was discussing the many contributions that he had made to our business. He took one hundred percent credit for everything positive that had happened during the period he worked there, sharing credit with no one. His perception of his contribution differed greatly from that of anyone else who worked with us at the time. His ego had greatly inflated his sense of accomplishment to ridiculous proportions."

"Don't take Me wrong, Jim," the Voice clarified, "to be successful in business and in life you have to have a healthy appreciation of your abilities. But you also need to be aware of your limitations. Your ego is like a tire. When it is properly inflated it runs along the road smoothly with little damage to its tread. When it is over inflated or under inflated it wears out much more quickly and never gives you a smooth ride. It is a wonderful thing to be sure of one's self, but not a good thing to be full of one's self.

Jim had a puzzled look on his face as he strained to understand. "But doesn't that sometimes require walking a fine line?"

"Not if you make it a point to never be too self-important to listen to others around you," the Voice explained. "Too often people think that they are listening when they actually aren't at all. Remind yourself regularly, Jim, to be a good listener."

"How do I..."

"Look into their eyes if you can," the Voice said, anticipating Jim's question. "Look at the expression on their face, and see what their body language is telling you. Try to sense their feelings. Don't just listen to their words—*hear* their voice! Always try to put yourself in their shoes."

"You just reminded me of a book that my wife and I used to read with our boys when they were much younger." Jim became more animated as he grabbed the top bar of his bike frame with both hands, leaned his weight into it, and began to rock back and forth. "It was called *The New Ears* and was written by a Danish women named Anne de Graaf. We would often feel that our boys were not listening and they told us that we did not always listen to them either. We realized that they were right. In the book, a little girl named Julie made a set of big purple ears out of construction paper for all the members of her family so that they could wear them when they needed to listen better to each other. When a family member put on a set of the purple ears it meant that they didn't feel like they were being heard."

The Voice's eyes sparkled watching Jim, totally absorbed in his story.

"I sometimes wish I could make sets of purple ears for everyone at work," Jim said more to himself, "I'll bet that'd be an effective way to let people around you know that you don't feel like they're listening to you—just put on your big ol' purple ears."

"Even those that many consider to be experts in a particular field have something to learn from listening," the Voice asserted. "There is always a reason to listen. There is always a reason to be interested in those around you. When you show interest in others they are much more apt to show interest in you."

"I used to be a much better listener. I really could use those purple ears," Jim nodded, his mind far away. He was still rocking back and forth, and this time he leaned a little too far forward and almost fell over, awkwardly recovering his balance. "Hey, that wasn't my fault," Jim blushed.

The Voice grinned broadly. "You just fell into the next lesson you need to learn."

Jim smiled sheepishly. "Can't there ever be an *easy* way to learn a life lesson?"

"It's important to keep your pride in check and remain humble," the Voice said earnestly. "Pride causes people to do almost anything to avoid looking bad."

Jim righted his bike and shook off his embarrassment.

"If you make a mistake, admit it. Don't try to blame someone or *something* else," the Voice emphasized. "If you owe someone an apology or a thank you, give it to them. Don't be above any task. Don't be above anybody. Think of those around you more, and of yourself less. Gain wisdom through humility by soaking up knowledge from everyone around you. Many wonderful lessons in life come from places we never expected them to, but you will not learn them if you are not listening."

"Standing here in this beautiful place, I do feel humble," Jim declared. "I feel like I just opened up a door to my mind. I have so much to learn and I have inadvertently kept the door locked. I hope that it will never happen to me again. I want to learn something new each and every day of my life. I have been in too big of a hurry. I have failed to truly listen to those around me and I have missed so much of what life has offered me. Now I understand that everyone around me is precious and has a unique voice and message."

Jim gave the Voice a grateful smile. His expression then took on true humility as he reached for his kickstand with his foot and gave it a flick. "I have to head home now and get ready for my son's soccer game later today—and tomorrow is a very special day for you. Can, I mean, *may* I see you again, Monday morning in the car?"

"Have a wonderful weekend with your family, Jim, and I will see you then." The Voice leaned over to smell a flower. In an instant they were one and the same.

"Take my yoke upon you and learn from me."
Matthew 11:29

"Let the wise listen and add to their learning."
Proverbs 1:5

Chapter Eight - BALANCE

"My father always reminded me that I should enjoy life, and he practiced what he preached. No matter how hard he worked, he always made sure to leave enough room to have a good time." - Lee Iacocca

<u>Wesley's Rule</u>
"Do all the good you can,
By all the means you can,
In all the ways you can,
At all the times you can,
To all the people you can,
As long as you ever can."
- John Wesley

The remainder of Saturday, then Sunday passed quickly. Jim's mind continued to buzz as he thought about everything that had happened to him the week before. It was hard to believe that his life could be so different in just seven days. Monday morning arrived and Jim was backing his car out of the driveway, starting his drive to work.

"Good morning, Jim."

Jim looked over and saw that his new Partner was materializing in the passenger seat.

"It's the start of a whole new week. What's on your mind this morning?"

"I've been doing a lot of thinking," Jim said, giving it a little gas and frowning at the sluggish response, "and I realize that I've really let my life get out of balance. My life has become about my job and to a lesser degree about my family. I have lost touch with many of what used to be my closest friends, I have not been active at all in my church, I attend only some of my kids' activities, and I am really not involved in any other clubs or organizations other than those directly tied to my business.

"It's good that you are seeing this." The Voice's eyes were reassuring.

Jim continued to pump the gas pedal until the engine finally picked up. "The word that keeps popping into my head is *Koyaanisqatsi*, which was the name of a very meaningful movie I saw about twenty years ago. It's based on a Hopi Indian word, which means 'life out of balance.' Without realizing it I have let my entire life get totally out of balance."

"Don't be so hard on yourself," the Voice admonished softly. "The biggest step is recognizing this—and then starting to do something about it. You are absolutely right. Your life has been very much out of balance and now you just need to start doing something about it."

"Haven't I already done the *starting* part?" Jim asked, a bit troubled.

"Yes you have," the Voice agreed. "You have a new attitude at work, and as a result you are being more productive in less time. You are spending more time with your family, and you are getting out more to exercise. So you are off to a good start. As the old saying goes, 'no one ever wished on their death bed that they had spent more time at work.' You're beginning to apply the concept of 'work smarter and you won't have to work harder.' It's always a good idea to take time to plan out your next day or the upcoming week."

"You know, I used to," Jim said, heaving a ponderous sigh.

"Jim, you have to be truthful with yourself. If you are cutting back at work because you no longer like your job, that is not finding a balance in your life, that is just running away from your real problem. Balance is about finding joy and fulfillment in your work life *and* your personal life. Plan more family events. Set aside times each week to call up friends and former business associates and keep up with their lives. Get more involved in your church again. Put your skills to good use. Join a health club or plan more regular times to exercise. Eat healthy foods. Take the time to lose the twenty pounds that you need to take off."

Jim did a double take. He took a deep breath and unconsciously sucked in his gut as he passed the school crossing.

"Take your wife out on a *date* more often. Your family, your church and your friends are the support structure that you have around you to help you live your life in the most constructive way possible. You must always keep your support structure strong. Surround yourself with friends who help you to be better and stronger. What would happen if you lost your job? Who would be there to support you? You must always look to broaden your horizons and to make yourself into a more complete person."

Jim was entering the freeway now. It was the usual Monday grind and he had to battle his way into the congestion. "I remember reading an article a while back from *Time Magazine* on the Internet about a book called *Wedded To Work*. It talked about how workers in our generation often measure success by how much we work. We are working longer and longer hours and have become emotionally wrapped up in our jobs. When a job ends for whatever reason, people are finding that they have nothing to fall back on. Their jobs have become their lives and they simply don't know how to act when they don't have their job anymore. Even without losing a job, workers suffer today because we sacrifice our families, our friends and much more to spend more time at our jobs. It is an alarming trend!"

"When work becomes your whole life you really don't have much of a life at all."

"It made me stop and think," Jim said, welling with emotion, "you know, I haven't even spoken with my college roommate in over two years. He was the best man at our wedding and one of my oldest and dearest friends. I have simply forgotten about many of the people that I have been closest with in my career as well. I don't spend nearly enough quality time with my wife and kids and I only get any real exercise once or twice a month. I know that I have gotten better lately, but that is not good enough."

"Beyond work, you always have to remember: faith, family and fun." The Voice rose in timbre, "you must remember that you are also here to enjoy life and to grow as a person, not just to struggle and survive. There is no reason to rush through life. Find diversions that help you to have fun. Even changing simple routines like driving home a different way some nights will give you some needed change. Your idea of going to the park at lunch is a good one. Get away to think sometimes. Invite others to join you. Talk about your favorite sports team or the last book that you read or a good movie that you have seen. When is the last time that you read a book that wasn't about business?"

"Let's see… how old are you?" Jim joked. He then blushed, realizing he really couldn't remember.

"Charge your battery! Count your blessings! When is the last time that you went out with some friends to just relax and not have the conversation dominated by work?"

The question caught Jim speechless, knowing the Voice had pegged him, albeit kindly.

"Remember that you are not on this earth only to earn a paycheck and to accumulate things, but to make the world a better place for this generation and those to come."

"It is getting clear to me now," Jim recovered, speaking confidently now, "the key to all of this is finding the balance between being a successful businessman, a good father, and a person of faith."

"Putting it all together is not easy," The Voice allowed. "There's the fear of losing your job. The fear of not being able to support your family. The fear of failure. The uncertainty of the current job market with massive layoffs being announced in many industries, even in companies that you thought it could never happen to."

"Not to mention the incredible rash of improprieties at Fortune 500 companies that seems to have no end."

"All of these things contribute to offsetting your balance."

"Well, you've given me another thing to think about now. I have to balance my life in my own way." Jim couldn't believe he was suddenly heading down the exit ramp. Where had the time gone in all that congested traffic?

"Watch out for cross traffic," the Voice cautioned, ever so subtly shifting his gaze up ahead.

"Man! We're almost there," Jim looked perplexed as he gestured toward his office building just up the street. "Once again, I thank You for taking all of this time with me."

"I'm just doing what you called me here to do."

"I can't believe the change that You are making in my life. Really, thanks!"

"You are very welcome," the Voice said, and continued in the most incredibly understanding tone that Jim had ever heard. "The fact is, I have *always* been here for you. You just didn't choose to see me."

Jim was uncertain how to respond.

"Everyone can lead a fun and fulfilling life. It is just a matter of what glasses you choose to view your life through and the attitude that you have about your life. You have chosen to see things differently. Congratulations!"

Jim brightened at the compliment. "Tomorrow I have to go out of town on business. Is there any chance we could we meet at my hotel tomorrow night?"

The Voice began to disappear. "I'll look forward to it, Jim."

"...ask where the good way is and walk in it and you
will find rest for your souls."
Jeremiah 6:16

Chapter Nine - REINVEST

"We make a living by what we get, but we make a life by what we give." - Sir Winston Churchill

"What you keep to yourself you lose, what you give away, you keep forever." - Axel Munthe

The long day of travel, meetings and a late dinner with many business associates was over. Jim went to his hotel, took the elevator up to his room and went inside. He was relieved to see the Voice already sitting on the couch, waiting for him to arrive.

"Hello, Jim," the Voice said pleasantly, "what is on your mind today?"

As a reflex, Jim loosened his tie with one hand and headed straight for the mini-bar, setting his briefcase down on a barstool. After grabbing a tall glass and filling it with ice, he started to reach for one of the small liquor bottles, then stopped short. He grabbed tonic water instead.

"It's good to see you," Jim sighed, filling up his glass. "Thanks to you my mind just continues to race with new ideas. Today I flew here with several people who work for me, and was in a meeting with many more junior people from my company's affiliates. All of them were listening intently to everything I said and many were clearly looking for my guidance and direction."

"Congratulations, Jim," the Voice said with utmost sincerity. "You are like a beacon of light now. You are very powerful."

"Thanks," Jim said humbly. "Anyway, it made me think about a feature I saw on television several years ago during the NBA Basketball Finals when the LA Lakers met the New Jersey Nets. It was with Kobe Bryant, one of the biggest stars in the NBA—a man with unlimited talent, tremendous poise, and a great presence. He was drafted out of high school and spent the early years of his career at the end of the bench, not getting into games very often. His main opportunity to grow was during practice sessions. He explained in the interview that Byron Scott, who was then the coach of the Nets, and was formerly a veteran guard for the Lakers, spent countless hours both on and off the court teaching him about the game. Kobe credited Byron Scott for having a major impact on his life and his career. Even a superstar starts out young and inexperienced and needs to be nurtured. And because of his kindness and compassion for a younger player, the legacy of Byron Scott lives on with the Los Angeles Lakers. This made me think of my own career..."

Yes," the Voice agreed, "That is a very good analogy."

"Even now, I still seek out the guidance and advice of those who have mentored me in the past. But the Kobe Bryant story made me realize how selfish I have been. I have thought of myself as a giving person, but I clearly am not. I don't reach out to others the way I should. I have learned so much that I could pass on to others and I rarely do it, even with my own direct reports."

"You've just acquired something of great value," the Voice said, enthralled with Jim's progress. "Teaching and supporting others helps *you* to learn and grow. It is much like planting a seed and then watering it to make sure that it grows. The crop that you yield will help your heart and compassion grow even more. Many people grow only perennials in their gardens because they see the fruits of their labors year after year. Any good you do will always come full circle back to you. Plant the seed with kindness, wisdom and knowledge; water it with reinforcement, trust and responsibility, and you will grow a tall and healthy evergreen."

Jim nodded enthusiastically and raised his glass in a gesture of acknowledgement.

"Be there for those around you. Those who work for you, those you work with and those you work for. They may not need to learn anything more than that they have a friend who is there for them. They may only need support."

"Yes," Jim said intently, "I think I understand."

"Reinvesting in others is about being there for others, no matter what assistance they might need. Remember Jim, reinvesting goes beyond work. You must also reinvest in your world with your time, effort and money."

"For example?"

"Remembering the homeless by volunteering at a shelter, coaching a Little League team, or visiting a shut-in neighbor are all means of reinvesting in your world. Donating money to your church, a charity foundation, or any other worthy organization is also part of reinvesting. Everyone on this earth must reinvest to make this world a better place, today and for the centuries to come. Fulfilling your purpose that you shared with me last week is a wonderful way to reinvest."

"Now I understand," Jim said with heartfelt conviction.

"Also remember that one of the greatest ways to support someone is to pray for them."

"I promise You that from this day forward," Jim said, tipping his glass as if making a toast, "I will do my best to reinvest in my career, the people around me, and in the world." Jim took a drink. "I am glad that you brought up prayer. The thing that has amazed me the most this past week is Your direct response to my prayer. I have been overwhelmed by this."

"As I said, I always answer every prayer, but in *My* own way," the Voice resolved.

"This morning as I packed to leave on this trip I picked up some magazines that I hadn't read and happened to pull this month's edition of the *Daily Word* out of a drawer in my desk. I put all of these in my briefcase to read on the plane. I have had a subscription to the *Daily Word* for more than ten years and really don't read it that often anymore. Today for some reason I chose to read it on the plane."

"As I knew you would." The Voice appeared to wink.

"Today's daily word was to 'Pray For Others,'" Jim smiled back. "Here, let me read the page for you, it is right here in my briefcase."

Jim popped the latches on his briefcase and removed the magazine, already open to the appropriate page. "*'My prayers do not change God; my prayers change me by changing my attitude to align with the divine plan. Prayer is the means by which I adjust my perception to see the good outcomes ahead for myself and others.*

"*'I do not plead with God to change a situation. I affirm that the loving presence of God is active in and through my life and in and through the lives of those for whom I pray. I don't claim to know what is best for them, but I know that God does.*

"*'I pray for others purposefully and positively. Like brilliant beams of sunlight reflecting off a mirror, my prayers for healing shine out to enfold and comfort the people who are close to me and those who are far away.'"*

Jim closed the magazine and returned it to his briefcase. "This passage has taught me one of the greatest lessons of my life. In addition to being generous to people with myself and my gifts, to reinvest in people by praying for them is clearly one of the most important things that I can be doing."

"Jim," the Voice's expression turned very serious, His tone impassioned, "this is something that cannot be taught, it has to be experienced—the incredible power of prayer. It is a tool with limitless power. The most important advice that I can give to you is to pray from your heart and to pray often. Pray for those you love and even for those you hate. Do not be stingy with prayer. Pray for your family, your co-workers, your neighbor, your friends and those on the other side of the Earth. You can never pray too much! Reinvest in others and you will see the results very quickly. I must be leaving now, Jim. You must rest for your long day tomorrow."

"Thank you, you obviously know me well." Jim emptied his glass, then walked over and dropped down on the opposite couch, facing the Voice. "I am very tired and I have a lot to think about once again. Will you ride with me to work on Friday morning after I return home?"

"I will see you then, Jim," answered the soothing Voice. "Peace be with you."

Jim rubbed his tired eyes with the palms of both hands for a second. When he removed them, the other couch was empty. But Jim could still feel His presence everywhere in the room.

"One man gives freely, yet gains even more; another withholds unduly; but comes to poverty. A generous man will prosper; he who refreshes others will himself be refreshed."

Proverbs 11:24-25

"...pray for each other so that you may be healed. The prayer of the righteous is powerful and effective."

James 5:16

Chapter Ten - GRATITUDE

"Feeling gratitude and not expressing it is like wrapping a present and not giving it." - William Arthur Ward

"Gratitude unlocks the fullness of life. It turns what we have into enough, and more. It turns denial into acceptance, chaos to order, confusion to clarity.
It can turn a meal into a feast, a house into a home, a stranger into a friend. Gratitude makes sense of our past, brings peace for today, and creates a vision for tomorrow." - Melody Beattie

Jim was still a little tired after his trip, but he got up and went through his normal ritual, pouring himself a cup of coffee, but this time he paused to kiss his wife and kids goodbye, and then was off to his car. He backed out of the garage, into the street, and started his drive to work.

"Good morning, Jim," the Voice was robust. "Did you enjoy your trip?"

"It's always great to be home," Jim admitted, "but the good thing about traveling is that it gives you a lot of time to think."

"What have you been thinking about?"

"I have been thinking about how lucky I really am," Jim replied. "I have a wonderful wife, two great children, good health and a great job, and most importantly, I have You."

"You are a very lucky man," the Voice offered modestly.

"The challenge now is remembering that *all* of the time," Jim said, slowing down in anticipation of the school crossing guard.

"You must maintain your feeling of gratitude during times of adversity and pain," the Voice affirmed.

"I certainly didn't feel gratitude when my father passed away." Jim's expression clouded. "I certainly didn't feel gratitude when I was in a bad car accident, when I lost a lot of money in the stock market, or when I lost out on a big real estate deal…"

"But you should have," the Voice interjected matter-of-factly.

Jim shook his head in disbelief as he slowed to a stop. This time children were crossing. "I, I don't understand!?"

"You should be thankful that your father lead a long and happy life and that you had thirty-five years to spend with him," the Voice patiently explained.

"That's true," Jim nodded, "my best friend in college lost his dad when he was only ten."

"You should be thankful that you were able to walk away from your car accident."

"Actually," Jim became more animated, "that broken arm got me back into reading some really inspiring works of literature. I was spending way too many late evenings playing video-golf on my computer."

"And you should be thankful that you could afford the money that you lost in the stock market, and lost in commissions."

"I get it!" With the kids safely across, the crossing guard waved her hand and Jim accelerated. "Out of every adversity, there is always something to be grateful for."

"But few people have the presence of mind to sift through the bad in order to find the good that is always there. Good and bad always coincide. It's up to you where you put your focus."

Jim's head was spinning. It was like a light had suddenly turned on.

"Gratitude makes you happier and healthier," the Voice went on. "When you are filled with gratitude you are also filled with peace, and being at peace is a much more wonderful way to live."

Jim sailed up the onramp.

"No matter what is happening in life, there is always something to be thankful for. You are wise to never take the good in your life for granted, because things can change quickly. Life is much more fulfilling when you focus on what is right instead of what is wrong."

Jim merged into the surprisingly light Friday traffic.

"The best advice that I can give you is to take time each day to think about the wonderful things in your life that you have to be grateful for."

"But it's not easy to remember to do this." A large black car was crowding Jim, but backed off at the last second.

"Then every time that you think of something that you are grateful for, record a voice memo on your mobile phone, write yourself a note on your computer or PDA, or even do it the old-fashioned way and write yourself a note on a piece of paper and put it in a file," the Voice proposed.

"I can do that," Jim declared excitedly. "Any other suggestions?"

"Yes," the Voice went on, "the best way to think about it is how much you would miss something if it were no longer in your life."

Jim merged into the fast lane.

"Call it your 'Gratitude File.' Make a point to add something to it regularly. It can be as simple an item as the weather."

"I like Your idea and I will do it." Jim was so exhilarated he accidentally hit the windshield wiper arm—or was it an accident? After a couple of rapid swipes he disabled it.

"But don't just put things in your file that you have to be grateful for each day." The Voice gave no sign He had anything to do with the errant wiper. "Also write down the *people* that you are grateful to—and how you plan to thank them."

"Good point. I realize that I don't take the time to really thank the people that I count on the most."

"Sure," the Voice acknowledged, "most people say 'thank you' and are often respectful, but that really isn't enough."

"I know what you mean," Jim winced, glancing in his rearview mirror to change lanes. "I can't remember the last time I brought my wife flowers or planned a special time away with her to thank her for standing behind me, for all of these years together, and for being such a great mother and a great person."

"Who else?"

"It's been more than a year since I treated my secretary to lunch or went out of my way to do something special for her."

"And…" the Voice prompted.

"I have many tremendous people working for me and supporting me and I don't really extend myself to them. But

I am going to change that." Jim tagged his steering wheel with a determined fist.

"If you can't shake someone's hand and say thank you in person, send a 'Grati-Gram'. This is a digital age. You can send an e-mail or an IM or leave a voice mail for anyone at any time. Even the simplest acknowledgement means so much." The Voice's expression was as gentle as ever.

"You're right, what's so hard about that? But I've always been so caught up in my own silly *stuff*, I just haven't given any thought to what they're going through." Jim headed down the exit ramp. "And come to think of it, my employers have given me this opportunity to build a wonderful career. Am I really grateful? Or have I just acted like they owed it to me because of all I've done for their bottom line? I need to e-mail them a 'thank you'."

"I'd say your eyes are really opening wide."

"I realize I have to show my gratitude to everyone who has been there for me. I know how much it means to me to get recognized for a job well done. It makes me want to work even harder next time."

"Gratitude is a way to fully participate in your world." The Voice became more intense. "Do you now see how powerful gratitude can be?"

"To me Oprah Winfrey is one of the greatest role models for the power of gratitude," Jim said as he waited for traffic to thin so he could turn right.

"Please tell me more," the Voice prompted.

Jim went on. "She came from very humble upbringings and had to overcome much hardship in her life. Along the way her grandmother, her father and key people such as Mrs. Benton, her fourth grade teacher, and a young counselor at the Boys and Girls Club, had an incredible effect on her life. Her profound gratitude for those who assisted her in life helped inspire her to become one of the greatest philanthropic givers of all time. In his book, *Giving*, Bill Clinton asked her why she started the Angel Network, and another charitable organization, the Oprah Winfrey Leadership Academy for Girls. She answered 'I wanted to give back what I was given, a sense of worth, everyone wants to matter.'"

"I remember that well," the Voice mused.

"I have respected her even more ever since."

"Good for you," the Voice nodded imperceptibly. "Everyone should remember those who supported them and show their gratitude. It is the right thing to do."

"I must never forget that I have You to thank for everything!"

"And thank you for your thankfulness."

Jim pulled into the parking lot. "Once again the time just sped by. Here we are at work already. When do you think we should we meet again?"

"Jim, I think that you need some time to absorb all that we have talked about during the last several days," the Voice announced pleasantly. "I think it best that we talk again in a week."

Jim wished it could be sooner, but he knew better than to question *this* Authority. So he just flashed a quick smile and said, "You're the Boss."

The Voice returned a reassuring smile. "I predict that this will be a very special week for you, and I will be excited to hear what you have to say."

"I will see you next Friday, then." Jim took a deep breath and let loose a hopeful sigh as he got out of his car and walked into his office.

"O Lord my God, I will give you thanks forever."

Psalms 30:12

Conclusion - STARTING LIFE ANEW

"And the end of all our exploring will be to arrive where we started and know the place for the first time." - T. S. Eliot

"You will be able to find Me at all times and in everything you are doing. It does not matter what chaos and confusion are all around you or what outer noise there may be." - Opening Doors Within

A week had passed. It was early Friday evening and although it had been a very busy week, Jim was running on reserve energy as he backed his car out of his parking space at work and started his drive home. As he looked left before making the right turn out of the lot, he heard a Voice that sent a shiver of excitement throughout his entire body.

"You look wonderful, Jim, it must have been a good week for you."

Jim quickly glanced over and gave the Voice a grateful smile. "Good doesn't begin to describe it! I feel like I have been filled with helium or something. I feel like my life has purpose now."

The Voice was pleased. His expression was like a beacon.

"I now am not afraid to leave the road if it is not going in the direction that I know You would want it to. I can't thank You enough for all that You have done for me," Jim raved as he turned on his headlights.

"Jim, you are capable of great things," the Voice avowed. "I am very proud of you. Tell me about what you have been doing."

"I have been working on the plan to accomplish my purpose that we discussed last week. I have put together a To-Do list, which I now need to expand upon. I have a good start on it, but it still needs some work. So far I have bought an exercise bike, which I have used twice already, I brought my wife flowers and booked a weekend in New York City for just the two of us next month. I want to fully explain to her what has happened in my life. I am taking my boys camping this weekend. I called my minister to volunteer more of my time, possibly as a trustee of my church. I took the time to listen to each person who works for me, to better understand what they were feeling. I say hello with a big smile to the receptionist, the janitor, and to everyone around me. I was enthusiastic and supportive and did not compromise my integrity once, even when I was facing a few very difficult situations. Not only that…"

"There's more?" the Voice asked spiritedly.

"I'm just getting started!" Jim said as he crested the onramp. "I shook his hand and thanked the elderly night guard in the lobby for his contribution to our company. I called my college roommate and we are going to get together in a couple of weeks. Most importantly though, I accept that I am a very lucky man with everything in my life to be thankful for—and I remind myself of all my blessings every night before I go to sleep."

The Voice appeared to raise an eyebrow. "You realize you have created a responsibility for yourself that you may not have intended."

"Bring it on!" Jim said as he merged smoothly into the fast lane.

"I am counting on you to inspire others, Jim," the Voice said, radiating confidence, "as I know you will."

"I won't let you down."

"Yes, I know." The Voice's eyes glimmered brilliantly. "And that is why I came to you—that was My reason for communicating with you in this apparent human form."

"Why do I feel you knew all along how things would turn out?" Jim said with a sly smile.

"Yes, I do have a tendency to know these things." The Voice lifted His eyebrows ever so slightly.

"Do you *always* know how things are going to turn out?"

"Technically, yes," the Voice turned serious, "but my gift to all of you is free choice. At any point in time you can shift off of one path you're following and onto another. That way, occasionally, I can be surprised."

Jim was astounded that the exit ramp for home was suddenly upon him. He eased on down it and came to a stop at the bottom. To his surprise, there were no other cars behind him. So he decided to take advantage of this opportunity and pulled his car off to the side of the road.

"I would like to show you something." Jim unhooked his seatbelt so he could reach into his back pocket and remove his wallet. He opened his wallet and removed a folded piece of paper, then buckled back up and headed for home. Jim gave the paper a shake and it unfolded. He put it on the right armrest, and pressed the creases flat with the palm of his hand. "The other night, I sat at my desk at home and wrote this. I typed it on my computer and printed it out on this small piece of paper so I can keep it in my wallet. I plan on reading it to myself each day."

In literally a blink, Jim found himself home. But he was starting to get used to these odd lapses in time.

"Please read it to Me," the Voice said.

Jim put the gearshift into Park, turned off the engine, clicked off the headlights and clicked on the interior light. He cleared his throat, then held the paper in front of him and began to read. "It's titled, *Carpooling With God.*"

At first Jim was a little self-conscious, but soon his voice resonated with a heartfelt pride.

"Dear God:

"Once again today I dedicate my life to You.

"Thank You for all of the many blessings that You have bestowed upon me and for being the driving force in my life.

"Today I start out fresh and new, free from my burdens of yesterday.

"No matter what comes my way today, I know that You and I together will handle it. Life is so much easier knowing that You are always there to counsel and guide me." Even with the interior light, Jim was having trouble reading the small print. The Voice sensed this and began to emit a glow, filling the car with just the right amount of light for Jim to comfortably see. He continued.

"Today, once again, I ask for Your guidance and Your help:

One: To remember my real *purpose* in life and to take full responsibility for my actions.

Two: To exhibit *integrity* in everything I do.

Three: To show real *commitment* and to work as hard as I can, always maintaining a positive attitude.

Four: To have *courage of conviction* in the face of adversity and to meet obstacles head on.

Five: To be filled with *enthusiasm* so that my energy can have a positive influence on all those around me.

Six: To always show *respect* for others, treating them the way I would want to be treated myself.

Seven: To show HUMILITY so as to listen and learn from all that goes on around me.

Eight: To maintain the proper *balance* in my life between work, family, religion, friends, leisure and community, and remembering to enjoy life.

Nine: To *reinvest* in others, sharing my experience, time, wealth and knowledge with those around me to help them also grow and prosper.

Ten: To feel and show GRATITUDE for all of the blessings and gifts that You have bestowed upon me.

"For all of this I ask Your help today dear Lord, so that I may better serve You through my benevolent service to others." Jim released an impassioned sigh and raised his eyes toward the Heavens. "Amen."

The Voice smiled beatifically and said, "Well put, Jim. Remember that I am always here for you. All you need to do is ask for My help."

"I will always remember that and will call upon You often." Jim put his hands together in prayer fashion. "I couldn't imagine it any other way. Thank you once again for everything."

"Good night, Jim," said the Voice. "Have a wonderful weekend with your boys. And Jim, always remember, that now that you have found Me, My light will shine on everything that you do. Truth and goodness are always there as your pillars of strength. You will be able to find Me at all times, no matter where you are or what you are doing."

Jim reached for the dash and clicked a switch. As the interior light faded out, the Voice vanished along with it. Jim was surprised by the sudden disappearance until he realized that a Glow remained. Not in the car, but inside of *him*. He could feel the light of God shining within, filling up his entire being.

Jim whispered "thank you" and could swear he heard "your welcome." But where did it come from? Not from inside the car? Suddenly it dawned on him who was speaking.

"Of course!" Jim nodded, "my inner Voice."

Jim smiled, opened the door of his car and went into the house knowing that his life would never be the same—and overwhelmingly happy that this was so.

"Ask and it will be given to you; seek and you will find; knock and the door will be opened to you. For everyone who asks receives; he who seeks finds; and to him who knocks, the door will be opened."

Matthew 7:7-8

SELECTED BIBLIOGRAPHY

Blanchard, Ken, and Norman Vincent Peale, *The Power Of Ethical Management*. New York: William Morrow and Co., 1988.

Buford, Robert P., *Halftime: Changing Your Game Plan From Success To Significance*. Grand Rapids, Michigan: Zondervan Publishing House, 1994.

Caddy, Eileen, *Opening Doors Within*. Scotland: Findhorn Press, 1987.

Clinton, Bill, *Giving, How Each Of Us Can Change The World*, New York, Alfred A. Knopf, 2007.

God's Little Instruction Book. Tulsa, Oklahoma: Honor Books, Inc., 1993.

Julian, Larry S., *God Is My CEO: Following God's Principles In The Bottom-Line World*. Avon, Mass.: Adams Media Corporation, 2001.

Pollard, William C., *The Soul Of The Firm*. Grand Rapids, Mich.: Zondervan Publishing House, 1996.

Sachs, Andrea, *Wedded To Work,* Time.Com: Time Magazine: September, 16, 2002, Vol. 160, No. 12.

Schuler, Robert H., *Believe In The God Who Believes In You.* Nashville, Tenn.: Thomas Nelson, Inc., 1989.

HOW YOU CAN CARPOOL WITH GOD

- Cut out or Xerox the following 2 pages.

- Fold it up and put it in your wallet.

- Read it once a day, every workday, at one of these times. . .

  o before you drive to work
  o while you *ride* to work
  o at your desk before you start your work
  o on a break
  o over lunch
  o immediately after you get home from work
  o anytime you need relief from stress at work

Carpooling With God.

Dear God:

Once again today I dedicate my life to You.

Thank You for all of the many blessings that You have bestowed upon me and for being the driving force in my life.

Today I start out fresh and new, free from my burdens of yesterday.

No matter what comes my way today, I know that You and I together will handle it. Life is so much easier knowing that You are always there to counsel and guide me.

Today, once again, I ask for Your guidance and Your help:

1) To remember my real PURPOSE in life and to take full responsibility for my actions.
2) To exhibit INTEGRITY in everything I do.
3) To show real COMMITMENT and to work as hard as I can, always maintaining a positive attitude.
4) To have COURAGE OF CONVICTION in the face of adversity and to meet obstacles head on.
5) To be filled with ENTHUSIASM so that my energy can have a positive influence on all those around me.

6) To always show RESPECT for others, treating them the way I would want to be treated myself.

7) To show HUMILITY so as to listen and learn from all that goes on around me.

8) To maintain the proper BALANCE in my life between work, family, religion, friends, leisure and community, and remembering to enjoy life.

9) To REINVEST in others, sharing my experience, time, wealth and knowledge with those around me to help them also grow and prosper.

10) To feel and show GRATITUDE for all of the blessings and gifts that You have bestowed upon me.

For all of this I ask Your help today dear Lord, so that I may better serve You through my benevolent service to others. Amen.

9 781604 778779